# Songs of the Shepherd

Hymns of Comfort and Safety

Arranged by
Jan Sanborn

*From the Hymns for All Seasons Piano Series*

# Foreword

The idea for this book, "Songs of the Shepherd" was borne out of a wonderful class I've been attending, taught by Irene Simmons, a gifted Bible teacher. Her sessions on the life of David, and particularly her relevant insights on the 23rd Psalm, have provided inspiration for my settings of these well-loved, beautiful hymns.

Additionally, given the current events, and the hostilities and anxieties surrounding them, we long for a place of safety and comfort. Where better to go than to the Great Shepherd?

On this collection you will find a potpourri of styles - from the simple Swedish hymn, "Children of the Heavenly Father," the flowing "When Peace Like a River," the poignant "Savior, Like a Shepherd Lead Us," to the gospel style of "Blessed Assurance."

May I make a few suggestions for performance?

1. In all of these the melodic line is paramount; shape it as though you were singing it. The accompaniment can be secondary, but there are some inner voice leadings that would be fun to bring out.

2. I would caution you to use the pedal judiciously, and to observe the dynamics and tempo markings. These will help to bring meaning to the pieces.

May you enjoy reading through this book, and find the learning of these beautiful hymns a truly comforting experience.

Jan Sanborn

Pianist Jan Sanborn is a musician whose versatility has enabled her to perform in a wide range of musical experiences -- as soloist, accompanist, and coach -- in both the classical and popular idioms.

Jan began playing for church at the age of six in Ames, Iowa. She began her piano studies at the Iowa State University, continuing at Drake University, Westmont College, and Cal State University Northridge.

As a published composer/arranger, she is a member of ASCAP. Her works can be found with a variety of publishers, and she has recorded three solo CD's.

Ms. Sanborn has performed as accompanist with the Roger Wagner Chorale on several of their Far East tours, with the Angeles and Pacific Chorales, and with the LA Chamber Singers. She is the choral staff accompanist at California State University, Northridge.

Jan has served as organist for leading Southland churches, and is the current President of the National Association of Church Musicians, formerly CCG. She is in demand as a clinician for music conferences and seminars, and has served as music director for various church and community productions.

# THE LORD'S MY SHEPHERD

JESSIE S. IRVINE
*Arranged by* JAN SANBORN

rall.
mf
a tempo
cresc. poco a poco
f
pp

50
mp
rall.
p a tempo
54
58
62
molto rit.
66
f
p a tempo
rit.

# SAVIOR, LIKE A SHEPHERD LEAD US

WILLIAM B. BRADBURY
*Arranged by* JAN SANBORN

14
mf
17
20
p
23
26
mp

29
32
35
f
38
mf
41
p

44
8va
mf
p
47
50
53

# LEAD ME, LORD

SAMUEL SEBASTIAN WESLEY
*Arranged by* JAN SANBORN

Variation I
Lightly
17
p
21
25
mp
29
33
Variation II
mf

37
41
cresc. poco a poco
45
f
mp
49
p
cresc. poco a poco
53
Variation III
mf

57
61
65
rit.
mp
68
gradually slowing to end
p

# JESUS, LOVER OF MY SOUL

JOSEPH PARRY
*Arranged by* JAN SANBORN

17
mf
mp
20
23
poco rall.
mf a tempo
26
8vb
29

32
mp cresc. poco a poco
35
f
38
mf
41
mp
44
f

47
50
53
p
56
p
59
molto rit.

# LORD, I NEED A SHEPHERD

*Music and Arrangement by*
JAN SANBORN

16
meno mosso
mf
poco a poco cresc.
20
f
24
rit.
a tempo
p
8va
28
32

36
molto rit.
with more movement
pp
p
39
mp
simile
42
cresc.
45
poco rall.
a tempo
f
48

51
54
rall.
a tempo
L.H.
R.H.
p
57
mf
60
pp
[ no ped. ]
63
rit.
pp

# BLESSED ASSURANCE

PHOEBE P. KNAPP
*Arranged by* JAN SANBORN

17
21
25
29
33

37
41
45
49
53
cresc. poco a poco
f

57
8vb
61
65
mf
69
gradually slowing to end
73
p

# HE HIDETH MY SOUL

WILLIAM J. KIRKPATRICK
*Arranged by* JAN SANBORN

20
rall.
a tempo
24
28
mf
32
37
dim. poco a poco
p

42
accel.
rall.
mp
46
50
cresc. poco a poco
54
mf
58
rall.
p
a tempo

62
67
cresc. poco a poco
mf
72
77
l.h.
r.h.
82

# WHEN PEACE LIKE A RIVER

PHILIP P. BLISS
*Arranged by* JAN SANBORN

**In a reflective mood** (♩ = 72)

13
16
19
23
26
rall.
a tempo

29
32
mf
35
Listesso
simile
38
41

44
47
2
50
Listesso
p
54
molto rit.
57
a tempo

# HIDING IN THEE

IRA D. SANKEY
*Arranged by* JAN SANBORN

13
16
piu mosso e cresc.
19
f
22
rall.
p
25
a tempo

28
31
34
37
41
mp cresc. poco a poco

45
mf
rall.
poco cresc. e accel.
49
rall.
p meno mosso
53
57
mp
p
gradually slowing to end
61

# WONDERFUL PEACE

W. G. COOPER
*Arranged by* JAN SANBORN

**With motion, in one** (♩. = 52)

23
28
piu mosso
32
poco cresc.
37
mf
mp
41

45
poco rall.
a tempo
49
53
57
61
rall.
a tempo

65
mf
69
Slower
dim.
pp
72
p a tempo
76
poco rall.
gradually slowing to end
80
8vb

# LIKE A RIVER GLORIOUS

JAMES MOUNTAIN
*Arranged by* JAN SANBORN

16
L.H.
L.H.
19
L.H.
22
25
mf
28

31
cresc.
8va
f
34
(8va)
37
mf
40
8vb
Listesso ♩. = ♩
pp
R.H.
44
mp
L.H.

47
mf
L.H.
Lightly
8va
mp
50
(8va)
53
(8va)
rall.
piu mosso
56
rit.
R.H.
cresc.
59
L.H.
mf

# CHILDREN OF THE HEAVENLY FATHER

Traditional Swedish melody
*Arranged by* JAN SANBORN

22
poco rall.
mp a tempo
26
cresc. poco a poco
mf
30
p
mp
34
38
poco accel.
poco rall.
mf

42
a tempo
46
50
cresc. poco a poco
54
pp
58
p
gradually slowing to end